I'm Not Fit

A Collection of "Healing Poems"
by a Survivor
for Rape/Incest Victims and Survivors,
and for Everyone to Enjoy

Mary Lee Adison

VANTAGE PRESS
New York

To my mother (succumbed to cancer from smoking)
my sister (succumbed to AIDS)
my fiancé (succumbed to murder)
Bill and Joe, who helped finance this book
my rapist perpetrator—he knows who he is

Contents

Preface

These poems are non-fiction. These poems are my life, and they represent over two decades of my experience with rape from the beginning to the present.

A vicious and malicious rape of the past leaves a vicious and malicious mental scar of today.

Acknowledgments

My acknowledgments are three-fold. Father, Son, and Holy Spirit.

While suffering silently for twenty-two years, I kept God at the forefront of my mind. I never forgot what He said, to have faith in Him and pray, and that I must wait on Him. He told me that He would not come on my time, but on His time. And the writing of this book is right on time. God as my co-author. Through my depression, He woke me out of a deep sleep, and I wrote down the words floating over my head, which formed these "healing poems." These poems are for you, sent down from Almighty God. When you read them once, you will want to read them over and over, and over again.

Introduction

To my readers:

My poems are:

Healing
Educational
Confronting
Entertaining
Respectable
True

So, "Come on out." Set your mind and soul free. My music and poems are for rape and incest victims and survivors, past and present.

They are also for the sexually harassed. They are for people thinking about raping someone, for people who have raped and have gotten away scot-free, like my perpetrator. For people incarcerated in jails and institutions for raping someone. For people in rehab for raping or engaging in incest with someone. For libraries and victim services.

For teachers, students, preachers, churches, children, ministers, priests, bishops, nuns, and anyone and everyone to enjoy. And lest we not forget, for our lawmakers, and for those who don't understand.

After reading my poems, I know that you will be refreshed, and I know you will return to them, because when you read them one time, you will want to read them over and over again.

Tell

I try to forget
I really, really do
But the flashbacks,
     the flashbacks
Are just too true

I try to forget
And since I didn't tell
I suffered every day
In a living "Hell"

My only sin
Was not opening my mouth
So now his memory
Follows me north to south

Never do what I did
Keeping it a secret
Always tell right away
This you won't regret

Tell, if he touches you
In your private places
Then you will be a winner
Jail, he'll have to face it

I was threatened not to tell
I believed his every word
I lived twenty-two long years
On those very words I heard

He took away my dignity
My self-esteem and hope
I'd reached the point of no return
The end of my short rope

I was threatened not to tell . . .

He wears a long black robe
A symbol of faith
But I know him better
As a man who has raped

I try to forget
I really, really do
But the flashbacks are just too true

Tell, I say, tell, if he touches you
In your private places
Then you will be a winner
Jail? He'll surely have to face it

Carpet of Fire

They laid a red carpet
To rest at his feet
They kissed his robe
A man so sweet

They prayed to God
To bless his soul
They worshipped him
As though he were gold

They never let
Him ever work
They never labeled
Themselves as "jerks"

They praised him
Raised him on pedestals so high
They made him feel
He could never die

But I alone
Know the truth
What he did to me
In his younger youth

I cannot erase
The days of yore
When he violated me
And left by the back door

He laid a carpet
Of fire for me
I have been burning
To let this thing free

Wherever I tread
My feet were burned
Now I share my story
'Cause I want you to learn

My carpet is clean now
Free from his litter
Free from his dust
And no more is bitter

Free to teach
And preach, and speech
Free to hold my head high
As I go down the street

Butterfly-Bee

He floated like a butterfly
He stung me like a bee
His wings were flapping vigorously
And his stinger was "third degree"

There was a struggle before the attack
But I was confused what to do
Never had no knowledge of how to fight
A man of God? This was new

There was a struggle of great proportion
A pushing, pulling, shoving match
A grasping, squeezing, bear-hugging thing
As he rubbed his penis behind my back

My fingernails scratched his face
Fighting? I didn't know how to hurt
In "those days" we did not know
And I paid a price in dirt

His stinger was "third degree" I claim
My third daughter carries his blood
I actually feel sorry for him today
'Cause his life is caked up with mud

Now, I'm the butterfly, and he's still the bee
I carry poems of joy and hope
I gather the sweet honey and gifts from God
The words, in these paragraphs for you to scope

Devil Incarnate

The devil incarnate
Most people don't see
I'm sad to say
My sister hates me

She told me she hates me
That she always did
I never suspected
But it was always hid

She broke my heart
She broke my trust
When she killed my man
With her friend of lust

They both did drugs
Two peas in a pod
And my life was changed
My man's life they robbed

God knows the man
Didn't deserve to die
But the Devil Incarnate
Had an evil eye

Still being a hypocrite
Still fooling the flock
But God will change things
"He's the solid rock"

Minimum Wage (Part I)

Minimum wage
Oh, what a rage
25¢ to copy this page

Minimum wage
Give us a break
$4.25 an hour
The pay that we hate

Have to buy toilet paper
Deodorant spray
Toothpaste a must
And soap for my face

Already $10.00
And no food in sight
Have to have carfare
To go to work tonight

$25.00 in tokens
First priority
Carfare these days
Is a luxury

Minimum wage
And taxes taken out
No need to brood
No need to pout

Dish detergent
To wash a plate
Krazy Glue
Whenever it breaks

No new dishes
In this pad
When rent is due
No more money I had

No money for movies
Or an extra job
I see why the young man
Feels he must rob

But that's not right
Will get you nowhere
May even lead to murder
And the electric chair

Minimum Wage (Part II)

Just hang in there
And don't give in
To temptation's lust
And earthly sins

Minimum wage
Can alter your mind
Even if they raise it
You're still not fine

90¢ a jump
Oh, what a joy
I can't buy my baby
A $10.00 toy

Pampers come first
Dryness is a must
If he gets a rash
Then I am crushed

Fee for a doctor
Money for some cream
Medicated powder
The "dream team"

Minimum wage
Your nerves on a perch
You need a new dress
To go to your new church

Salvation Army
Is where you buy your shoes
And some other things
To keep from crying the blues

Minimum wage
Oh, what a rage
In these days
Is abusive in ways

10

And this abuse
Leads to excuse
You must be strong
And do not use

Forty years and not a raise
There's something wrong I must say

Don't understand it
Never will
But minimum wage
Don't pay my bills

Mushroom

The secret was invisible to see
Then a pin dot, it came to be

Then it grew to the size of a dime
When I looked again, it was growing fine

Looked once more and I didn't believe
The secret so big, had to get out of me

It began to swell, my chest bust out
It pushed and pushed, I heard it shout

Mushrooming, mushrooming here and now
Never again to disavow

The secret hit the president's desk
And over in Rome, my letter rest

Cardinal O'Connor sent his reply
And it's heading for Congress, I'll get by

No more little secret, no shutting my mouth
It'll be heard from the north to the south

It's so big, and I am proud
If you're raped today, shout it out, and loud

Don't let no one tell you to shut your face
'Cause years on end, you'll be disgraced

Have the courage, I'll give you knowledge
Read these words on your way to college

Let no one touch you where the sun don't reach
I'll back you up, I'll preach and speech

I'll end this poem on this advice
Read my poems, and read them twice

Because

Because the rape was a minister's doing
I have not lost faith in God
It was the man with lust in his soul
Who felt that my body he had to rob

Because the rape was a minister's doing
Only made my soul cry out for help
Like a baby needs milk in a bottle
Like a dog needing a bone will yelp

Because the rape was a minister's doing
I always keep God at the front of my life
Raised my family, had my daycare
But I knew I'd never give up the fight

Because the rape was a minister's doing
I never could turn against my savior
The devil was in the man of God
Being raped, I feel, has done me a favor

I can teach others they must "tell"
To not hide it deep inside
To not feel guilty, or worthless
To not take twenty-two years to cry

'Twas the Day

'Twas the day of puzzlement
'Twas the day of confusion
'Twas the day of disbelief
And the day of "inclusion"

"Inclusion" with other victims
People afraid to talk
People afraid to be courageous
People who'll let rapists walk

'Twas the day of infamy
'Twas the day of lust and prey
And the day of trusting no more
Losing faith in the man that day

'Twas the day I'll never forget
It's etched into my brain
'Twas the day he was dripping wet
But I was not to blame

'Twas the day that changed my life
Never to be the same
'Twas the day of accomplishment
He won the molesting game

Not so fast, the years were slow
The mending was due to come
Out popped the truth, hiding no more
And I advocate to everyone

'Twas the day, long time ago
God said, "Let there be light"
And sure enough, I survived the ordeal
And "rape" is the war I will fight

The Threat

The threat was clever
The threat was insane
For twenty-two years I suffered
And he threatened me again

The threat was mixed
Into the sermon that day
No one else was aware of it
But it was like him calling my name

I knew it was for only me
As I had just been molested
The people sitting around in pews
Never dreamed, and never suspected

He must have thought
The previous night
What the sermon would be about
And he wisely gave it
Shoved it in my face
This man didn't want his people
To be visible and shout

He said he liked his women
To be pretty and attractive
To not wear nappy hair or Afros
Because they were distasteful

What could be more distasteful
Than a man who has raped?
What could be more disgusting
To lie about it at a later date?

If Walls Could See

We were comfortable and cozy
Until the Devil set in
He messed with my womanhood
He messed with my skin

He messed with my ears, my tits
And my neck
He messed with my head
It turned into a wreck

He messed with my soul
My heart, my mind
He messed with my clothing
My panties the last time

He messed with my faith
My self-esteem and dreams
He shut me out, then put me out
All I had was my kids, my only team

He messed with my privates
"If the walls could see"
They'd tell all that they saw
And my soul would be free

Down in the Subway

Down in the subway
Here I come
Move over vagrants
Move over bums

Down in the subway
My future gig
'Cause up here on top
I get no respect

Maybe down under
I'll be recognized
To be appreciated
To be obliged

Maybe down under
I'll get self-esteem
To come back up
To the streets of "mean"

Down in the subway
Can I survive
The test of time
Will it keep me alive?

No Need to Call Your Name

I don't need to say your name
You will know who you are
I do expect an apology
That's well overdue by far

But if you don't, well, that's OK
I didn't expect too much
From a man of yesteryear
Who touched what he shouldn't have touched

I don't need to call your name
I've given it to Jesus Christ
I've let go, and let God
I've called it more than twice

God will help me see it through
To ease the lifelong pain
Pain one can't see with the naked eye
The pain that's now caused *you* shame

I don't need to write your name
It's written in my prayer
Please let us forgive and forget
And heaven's gate, I'll meet you there

Some may say, leave that man alone
He's not bothering you
What they don't understand and see
The bothering is never through

Some may say, get on with your life
Do something to forget it
"Thanks" for giving me that good advice
Now I'll write it, and you can read it

Depression

Can't eat, can't sleep, can't concentrate
Can't mentally function right
Anxiety is always in your corner
You toss and turn all through the night.

Lonely and confused
You wish you had a friend
To stick it out with you
Until your journey's end.

You have no desire to go out
Your sex life has gone nil
You feel you have no hope
You feel life going downhill.

You cry and get in moods
Moods you can't understand
They swing back and forth
Dr. Jekyll and Mr. Hyde, "the Man."

Suicide may pick your brain
Dare you to be a fool
You should know better
You learned "not" in school.

You want to be alone
But you also want "out"
You feel life is worthless
You may go the wrong route.

You know there's a problem
Your intelligence tells you that
You want your self-esteem back
To get on the right track.

You search for an answer
You look for a solution
You need to find time
To make the right motion.

You're stressful, you're angry
You have no energy
You have guilt up to your neck
Not to mention, fatigue.

Your fears come out stronger
You have insecurity
You have all the signs of depression
You need a doctor, immediately. (Stat.)

The Gap

Twenty-two years is a very long time
To hold in a deep, dark secret
Can you imagine the mental impact?
The gap of time, one can't forget

Twenty-two years is a very long time
To hold back your life in shame
To be afraid to speak, come out in the open
And be afraid to mention his name

Twenty-two years is a very long time
To be imprisoned inside your body
Thank God for education, willpower,
Determination, bravery and lobby.

Twenty-two years is too long, my friend
Don't let it happen to you
Today we can tell, report, prosecute
The ball is in your corner to sue

If I'd told years ago
I'd be a millionaire
A DNA would prove his guilt
I'd be dancing on thin air.

But money isn't everything
Now, an apology would suffice
To put a closure to this chapter
To get on with my life

Why can't he help me accomplish this?
An "apology" is very much for him
I know he doesn't sleep at night
His getting into Heaven, is very slim

On Incest

Did your uncle, father
Cousin or brother, ever
Make you feel a little funny?

Did you ever wake up
Felt something strange
And it wasn't your toy bunny?

Did they ever touch
Your body parts
Over which you wear underwear?

Did they ever tell you
Look at "their privates"
And ask you to "touch them there"?

Did they tell you
Not to tell
They'd hurt you in some way?

Did they ever
Make you feel uncomfortable
As you look back on it today?

Sex with a loved one
In your family
Is not healthy
You should tell the police.

Sex with an uncle
Father, cousin or "bro"
Is just as carnal as a rapist on the go.

So, if you are molested
And afraid to tell
Ask God for courage and send him to jail.

Give Me Credit

Give the credit
Where credit is due
Give the credit
For telling the truth.

Give the credit
For sparing his life
Give credit
For not cheating on his wife.

Give me credit
For being morally right
And not being ashamed
To not give up the fight.

Give me credit
For not aborting my child
She came into the world
A victim all the while.

Give me credit
An apology is due
I write these words
To open the doors for you (Heaven's door).

I know you are out there
Feeling my pain
Let's all come together
Let's fight the shame.

Give the credit
Where credit is due
You're number one
Let your light shine through.

He Baptized Me

He baptized me in "Holy Water"
The pool, I was emerged
Woe unto me, I never dreamed
Months later, he had a bad urge.

He baptized me in "Holy Water"
God knew my heart was good
He saw the man putting my head under
He saw the abuse, I knew he would.

He baptized me in "Holy Water"
It felt so good to be free
Free of all sin, and wrong deeds
But Satan was after me.

Satan climbed into the man of God
Filled him with guile and lust
Stripped me from all my dignity
Took away my all, my trust.

I've been searching for an answer
Why me, Lord? Why not another?
I was afraid to tell anyone
Even my best friend, my mother.

The white sheet clung to my body
Like a second skin
As I emerged out of the pool
I'd be a victim of only him.

God knows my heart
God knows my plight
He's on my side
To win this fight.

It may not be in this lifetime
That I'll see victory
But I'll know in the afterlife
Will my abuser be there to greet me?

He baptized me in "Holy Water"
He raped me in human lust
He sued me to hide his guilt
He denied his child, his trust.

Your House or Mine?

Your house or mine?
Shall we set a date?
Should I brew some coffee
I can't hardly wait.

Your house or mine?
Makes no difference to me
I am not choosy
I like to be free.
My house or yours?
You can come over anytime
Don't take too long
Too long is like a crime.

Your house or mine?
It's been a long tiresome wait
It's worth the trouble
To not miss this date.

It's a long time overdue
It's two decades of delay
It has caused depression and stress
Let's get it over today.

Your house or mine?
Don't frown and don't grunt
Let's close this dreadful chapter
Come together and confront.

I've lost many nights
Of well-deserved sleep
I lost many dollars
Can't work, can't eat.

I've lost concentration
Self-esteem and hope
I've lost pleasure in sex
My life has lost scope.

No more sadness for me
I'm tired of solitude
No more the victim for me
Tired of being screwed.

No more sleepless nights
Tossing and turning and broods
No more fatigue syndrome
And no more bad moods.

Only positive thinking
So I can score
Score on succeeding
Nothing less, only more.

Grown Men Have Come Forward

Now grown men have come forward
About being molested also
When they were young altar boys
From their Roman Catholic priest they know.

The priest has admitted his guilt
Something the minister I know won't do
Can his heart be so cold and callous
As to lie in God's name untrue?

Can it be he has gone senile
Because of his advanced age?
I don't think so
He remembers everything else, I'm afraid.

Will you tell the truth, the whole truth, and
Nothing but the truth, so help you God?
States the man in the courtroom
He made a statement, denied everything
He will live in an eternal gloom.

Will he ever admit his guilt?
I'm sure his mind has re-entered the past
Of when he was a greedy man
A past that's resurfaced aghast.

I respect the priest who told the truth
He did not hide his terrible sin
He was a man, and stood up in shame
But he'll be pardoned by "God Supreme."

These men from the past
They cannot sue
Time has tarnished the crime,
These men from the past
They seek no vengeance
Just to tell their story from past time.

Grown men have come forward
They and I can relate
To this hideous, ugly crime
Of which now, the public hates.

Coming out of the Closet

Year after year, I wanted to be free
To stop hiding and get this devil out of me

Year after year, I nearly turned the knob
But I feared the man, half my life he robbed

Year after year, I tried to repress it
But the thoughts always surface, I could not suppress it

Year after year, anxiety building high
I wanted to scream to the far-reached sky

Year after year, the sight of him tore me
The thoughts of him, actually bore me

Year after year, eating me like a cancer
I looked and I looked, I had to find an answer

Year after year, it was locked up in my soul
Coming out of the closet, finally made me whole

Year after year, tormented all the time
I stayed in too long, and I paid for the crime

So now you see, I'm an advocate for thee
If you know someone has raped, don't let this man go free

The closet door is open, no more hiding inside
I came out too late, but I have my pride

Proud that I opened up and told family
Now I'm a teacher, to heal the ones like me

Proud that I opened up and made myself strong
And I'm proud, so proud, to sing my song

Year after year, no more hiding his lie
I came out of the closet, now it's his turn to cry

Confront Me

Will you confront me on your deathbed
Will you confront me on mine?
Why must we wait till we're sick and disabled
To wait till the end of our time?

Will you confront me in this life or not
'Cause I know I won't see you in heaven's nest
God will not let liars in
Nor rapists, nor murderers, unless they confess.

Why gamble on eternity
I know you've read my letters
I know you know I'm hurting inside
Why can't you make it better.

Why can't you simply apologize
Why can't you respect this victim
Why can't you shed some remorse
I feel like Job, and then some.

God knows your heart
And I do, too
Have you repented
It's the right thing to do.

I'm not condemning ministers
I'd marry one in a hurry
If God send one my way for marriage
My belly would be in flurries.

There's only one who violated me
I'm not changing the whole denomination
I just want justice, peace and love
And to erase my degradation.

Not There Yet

I cut off the phone and the answering machine
I do not answer the door
To go outside is a great effort
And to socialize is very poor.

I cut myself off to the outside world
Backyard picnics, barbecues, not for me
I feel I'm in a world by myself
Although I do have family.

I cannot, and do not show my face
Around their family table
I cannot go to family reunions
I feel I am not able.

All this is due to my not being healed
I am not all there yet
I feel everyone's goal is answered
But mine is still all wet.

I long for the day when I can be whole
To laugh and enjoy my full life
To catch up on what I've long missed
To have trust, then maybe be a wife.

I Have Forgiven Him

I have forgiven him
Because God forgave us first
But I long to confront
Like a mouth dry of thirst.

Like a desert needs sand
Like a lake needs water
Like a Christian preacher
You know that you oughta.

"Oughta do what?" you say,
You long know by now
You know like rain needs clouds
And like milk belongs to cows.

You know what you did
In the dark has now come to light
I'm sure not giving up
I will surely win this fight.

One way or another
I'll come out on top
'Cause God tells me to keep writing
Keep writing, and don't stop.

His hand leads my hand
His words flow like sweet juice
I keep buying more paper
I'll never stop its use.

I have forgiven him
'Cause God forgave us first
Why can't he respect me
Like I respect his church?

Sure, I left some papers
On some cars and on the doors
He cancelled my appointment
So, I had no choice.

My intention was to confront
My intention was good
So he can hold my hand,
Apologize like he should.

Are We There Yet?

Are we there yet?
Are our hearts clean and pure?
Can we honestly say
We'll walk through Heaven's door?

Are we there yet?
Have we all confessed?
Have we asked forgiveness
So we can help the rest?

Are we there yet?
Are you sure you're saved?
Double-check your heart
Before entering your grave.

Are we there yet?
Will we see Jesus?
Yes we will, if
Our hearts not devious.

Are we there yet?
Can we honestly say
That we can look forward
To a heavenly day?

Are we there yet?
Do some teach what they preach?
Or are they hypocrites
Hiding behind their speech?

Homeless

I feel like being homeless
A dreadful thought I admit
No place to comfortably rest your head
To brush your teeth or s——t.

I feel like being homeless
Put myself in other's shoes
Definitely a lowly place
To really sing the blues.

I feel like being homeless
To see underneath bridges and
To sleep in cardboard boxes
And sleep in crates and barges.

I feel like being homeless
They're many who are smart
Intelligent people mixed in the crowd
Who'll really break your heart.

I feel like being homeless
To meet men of the Vietnam War
To shake their hands, and pat their backs
For keeping us safe on shore.

I feel like being homeless
To meet all the victims here
Of cruelty, abuse, and bad times
To let them know I've been there.

No mailboxes filled with junk mail
No one to ring your doorbell
No one to break in your window
And frighten you, scared to hell.

No houses to get burned down
No dogs needed to protect them
No padlocks or burglar alarms
No bars on windows, and then some.

I feel like being homeless
To even up the score
To not pay rent, Ma Bell, and gas
To not pay Con Ed no more.

I feel like being homeless
But my family will never agree
They'd be out there, bringing me back so fast
So fast, I couldn't breathe.

I'm glad I have a support system
Who loves me and understands
And being homeless will not be needed
With this mom, with pen in hand.

Seatbelts

Hold me around my waist so secure
Prove to me, my life will endure

Taken from a crashed-up car
Totalled to the max by far

Snug your grip, and snap the click
Be on time for this dear miss

Three years or more, of thoughts bizarre
Three years of yearning, at most by far

They can save you in a car, or trap you in a fire or lake
Will they be my breakaway, will I make my big escape?

Seatbelts, the sound of safety, I love to hear the latch
There'll be no need for you to fear, there'll be no need for
    you to catch

"God" will protect me, He said He would
I'll follow His guidance, as I should

He said to believe and trust in Him
To pray and repent to avoid all sin

I love my Father, He's the greatest of all
I trust in Him, and I will not fall

He Lives with Me Every Day

Although he doesn't know it
He lives with me every day
Two decades plus, of fear and pain
From the crime in which he made.

He's constantly on my mind
He's constantly in my life
He's a chronic thought in time
My conflict in strife.

He's onto me like glue
He never goes away
I feel his hand, his breath, his teeth
Every God-blessed day.

He's with me in the morning
He's with me in the night
He's a computerized memory
He's always in my sight

He's entombed into my memory
He interferes with my train of thought
His elegant ghostly manner
I wish it could be caught

When will he ever go away
Taunting and haunting me every day
I'm sick, I'm weak, I'm weary,
From the crime in which he hath made.
And the crime in which I must pay.

I can't shake the flashbacks
I can't cover it anymore
God will help me in the end
Of this I'm very sure.

Why?

Why do you feel
You have to take it
Especially when it's not yours?

Why do you feel
No one will care
When we beg you "no," on all fours?

Why do you feel
You won't be caught
When it's just a matter of time?

Why do you feel
To come, see, and conquer
And not give a damn that it's mine?

Why do you feel
I'll give you power
I'll give you ego and control?

Why do you feel
You must take her self-esteem
And put her life on hold?

Why do you think
Rape is sex
When actually it's a crime?

Why do you take
A chance with your life?
Only you will pay the time

Why do you think
Rape is love?
You have no right to force her
Why do husbands
Feel the need
To subdue her and coerce her?

If she's a stranger
You have no right
To put your hands on another

Just like you have
No right, to have sex
With your sister or brother

It Never Goes Away

My hurt and pain
It never goes away
It lives with me
Every single day.

No one should have to go
Through what I did
It would have been different
If it wasn't hid.

It tore my life apart
It hid deep inside my soul
It lived in every vein and capillary
My pores, in every hole.

It rides me like a saddle
It's encased inside my brain
No doctor's scalpel can remove it
It's always there, the pain.

After he came, saw, and conquered
He nearly forgot his hat
A knock at the door startled him greatly
He ran out the door, and out the back.

He left me traumatized, dumbfounded, and confused
The faith in me was gone
He knew he committed a wrongful sin
He knew he did me wrong.

He's an Old Man Now

He's an old man now
Says his wife with pity
I remember him pulling, tugging,
Busting my bra strap, cupped my t——

He's an old man now
Basking in his glory
He never dreamed I'd come out
Of the woodwork, and tell my story

I've come back fully educated
And hoping to help someone else
'Cause I'd hate to see it happen to them
The ugliness that happened to myself

Did he think I faded away?
Did he think I died?
Did he think I'd never tell?
Did he think forever I'd hide his lie?

I feared he'd have a contract
Put out on my life if I told
So I never mumbled a single word
To any other living soul (until now)

It's too late for me to prosecute
It's too late to file charges
It's too late to sue
And I missed out on a million dollars

Only God knows the truth
He will be the judge and jury
He will bring the truth out
Because it's God's duty

Victim

I've been ridiculed and scorned
From the day that I was born
I've been falsely accused
Been mentally abused.

I've been tortured, I've been raped
I've been kept from total escape
I've been kicked to the ground
With a baby in my belly
I've been tossed and shaken
Like a bowlful of jelly.

I'm the victim of a murder
My kids must live in grief
Their father was brutally murdered
Taken from under his feet.

I've been conned for years
By a married man
Oblivion has taken my trust
Into "never-never land."

A thief stole my invention idea
He saw he could make a profit
I couldn't prove it then
And by then, I totally lost it.

So, people don't you worry
And loved ones, don't fret
I've a glorious day a-coming
And this you can bet.

After Suicide, the Pain Continues

Do you think taking your life
Is the end-all end?
I have news for you
News to think about, my friend.

If you are so selfish
To accomplish suicide
Did you ever think
Others would suffer, with you not by their side?

After you are gone, friends
Family members are left alone
To suffer in pain and grief
Until the cows come home.

How long will you make them suffer?
How long must they grieve?
Why must they endure this pain
Because you wanted to leave?

What you are doing
Is giving up your soul
Making the devil happy
Now he's got you in his hole?

There is one sin, my dear
That does not cover God's forgiveness
It is suicide
And it is everyone's business.

I Will Climb This Mountain

I will climb this mountain
The height of which I fear
Two things will come out of it
Either death or truth will adhere.

I gamble now, because he gambled
He gambled with mere words
He knew he had a case closed shut
When the threat was so real, that I heard.

Give my poems to those who care
Let them enjoy and look deep inside
Inside to see what was my struggle
To see, what years and years, I was forced to hide.

I will climb this mountain
Then maybe they will see
I had a problem I could not solve
Not myself, not I, nor me.

The courts don't know the depth
Of the hurt of which I feel
They'd have to live through it
To know the hurt is real.

Even today, some don't believe me
They wouldn't believe back then
Is this a helpless situation
Will this minister win again?

Can't Sleep

It is November 9, 1994
The day of my birth, could I ask for more?

It's a birthday, I've never seen before
God, grant me my life a peaceful score.

I can't sleep this morn, it is 4:10 A.M.
Can't sleep again
I toss and turn and shake
'Cause I'm thinking of him.

It is November 11
I think of the upcoming holiday
I don't think I can make it
Another season, he got his way.

It is November 13
How long will this go on?
I think of him in the night, in the waking morn.

It is November 14, 1994
Sleepless nights, circled eyes
My health is very poor.

I can go on, and on, and on,
The cycle never stops
I'm so tired in the P.M.
I could just fall down and drop.

This is not the only week
I've lost sleep in the night
It'll be three years Christmas Eve
The sleep fight of my life.

Dogged

He's been dogged for three years
As my secret bursted out
He's been as stubborn as a mule
And my message I will shout.

He's not yielding, neither bending
Like a tough piece of iron
He feels he's still master and king
Of the jungle, like a lion.

He has a tough coat of armor
Everything man makes, falls down
Soon, he'll be so soft like cotton
What goes around, comes around.

He can't dis me anymore
He can't dog me as he'd wish
He can't sweat me like a towel
He can't scale me like a fish.

He's been dogged for three years
He's refused my cries for help
Now, the Lord has instructed me
To get out and help myself.

Colors of Revictimization

Already abused and used, then, abused and used
by this new abuser, by this dark evil force with
power, I use the colors of the darkest side of the
rainbow, and dip them in coal and tar and ashes, to
reveal the dark, gloomy and dismal side of this heinous
    crime.

My heart was already bleeding, fast pumping and
jumping whenever the sound of the phone rings, or
someone rings the doorbell, and even a knock would
startle me. I lived with it every day.

Living in total denial, only haunted me more
each day, which passed into months, then years,
then decades, namely two. Those dark, dank, dingy
years that I suffered alone, while raising my
family alone, no one knew. Only my Lord and Savior knew.

God gave me the silver-streaked strength and the
colors of the rainbow. Etched with a gold lining.
He gave me the courage to come out of a "black on
black" mess, and confess. I prayed, and God
listened. I prayed, and God showered petals down
over me like a halo, with each leaf etched a poem.

"Revictimization" is a hell of a thing. Without the
grace and brace of God, I would not have survived
the mental torture. People say they're tired of
hearing about victim stuff all the time. Well,
victim stuff will always be here, whether they're
tired or not. Until all perpetrators are acknowledged,
past, present, and future, there will always
be "victim stuff," and the colors of revictimization.

Bad Toys

I am a big girl now
You are surely a big boy
You are older, wiser, and mature
Let's stop playing with bad toys.

Bad toys, like hiding and concealing
Bad toys, like ducking and lying
Bad toys, like sneering and snubbing
Bad toys, like continually denying.

Bad toys, like calling me a devil
Calling me ill-minded and vicious
Bad toys, like saying I'm not of God
And badly calling me malicious.

How can she turn his crime of the past
Turn it to make me look bad
I was traumatically damaged
I was traumatically mentally sad

He told me no one would believe me
And said my word would hold no ground
He told me I was less than he was
And until now, I couldn't come around.

Thank God our message has come out
Advocates and lawmakers please adhere
Please make our Congress listen
So past perpetrators, we'll no more fear.

Room at the Top

Is there room at the top for me?
You've been up there for years
Is there space, for sharing's sake?
Move over and let me see.

Is there room at the top for me?
Is there earth to go around?
Room to breathe, room to roam,
Is there room in your town?

So many wanting to reach the top
But only a few will make it
Is there room at the top for me?
Please say yes, and don't fake it.

I need to make my mark in life
God didn't want me to be silent
I need to open up and blossom
Full blooms, yellow, red, orange and violet.

Is there room at the top for me?
They say I can be anything I please
Are they saying it just to fool me?
Are they saying it just to tease?

I will wiggle and squeeze right in
I'm determined to not get gypped
I'll make my mark, I'll show them all
This pen and mouth will not be zipped.

Soaps

Can you wash off dirty lies?
Can I wash off stress?
Can you wash off scandalous truths?
I don't know, but I'll try Caress.

Can Palmolive clean an unseen scar?
Can Ivory be as pure as they confess?
Can soap and water be the answer?
Can it put this chapter to rest?

Can you scrub off all the pain
You caused my life to bring
Can I scrub off years of hurt
I'll try some Irish Spring.

Can you bathe away my loss
Can you bring back faith and love
Can I start all over?
Can I do it with some Dove?

Can you sponge away the illness,
The depression I feel every day?
Can I soak in future years
If I use some Coast or Camay?

Soap in your mouth
Will not make you come clean
I'll just keep asking with each letter,
Soap in your shower
Or bubble bath
Maybe just telling the truth will be better.

Blood, Sweat, and Tears

Alas, the blood did flow from my body
When the baby was sent from above
Before she was born, I knew not her father
Until I looked into her eyes with love.

Alas, the sweat did flow from my brow
Labor pains, contractions, sweating armpits
Dripping forehead, sweaty palms
Even my hair roots, and under my t——s.

Tears of pain, tears of joy
I wanted a baby boy
A girl would suffice
Alas, the rape haunted me all of my life.

I could not see abortion
As an ugly way out
So I hung in there
A lovely baby did sprout.

Now I ask you, Mr. Perp
Unless you are blind
This child looks exactly like you
What will you do to tie the bind?

Is God Trying to Tell Me Something?

How is it I can write twelve poems a night?
Is God trying to tell me something?
Why is it, I can't stop writing
The urge is so inviting.

How is it, my mind is consumed
With helping victims to heal?
Why is it, my typewriter sits
And waits for me to turn the reel?

How is it, the words just flow
Straight out, without my erasing a word?
How is it, I can write twelve poems
Of which no one has ever heard?

How is it, I can write many poems a day
Does God have plans for me?
Is it possible I can write a book
Or maybe two or three?

Oh happy day, oh happy day
Wouldn't it be a blessing
If I could see my books on a shelf
It would be quite honorably smashing.

I may have to self-publish myself
I can't afford "their" publication
One thing I know for a fact
Most poor folk can't make it in this nation.

$13,000 is a bit much for me
I don't even have $ one
So, I'll publish it myself
To see how much is my worth.

Can We Be Friends?

Can we be friends?
And call it a truce
After all, we have something in common

Can we be friends?
You never succumbed
To the fact that your child is a woman

Can we be friends?
I have crossed over
To be on the right hand of God

I hold my hand forward
I wave a white flag
I extend an invitation of love

Can we be friends?
My heart has softened
By chance, has yours softened too?

After all, I had your child
I couldn't believe it
But accepted it, why are you still blue?

You and I know
This is no show
But the curtain has fallen on me

I take my bow, and
Hold my head up high
I pray every day, you will see

I get on my knees
My candles are lit
And I feel your presence here

Can we be friends?
I ask you again
And friends beat enemies

Can we be friends?
We share a common bond
A child sent from Heaven to me.

Red Carpet Reversed

He was muscular and strong
I was skinny and weak
He was a football player
And he knew how to creep

Creep into the parish house
Where I found refuge
Little did I know
My vulnerableness he'd use

He was a smooth talker
A slick ladies' man
But I never told him
My body he could have

He thought every woman
Should kiss his feet
To roll a red carpet
When he walked the mean streets

Some men saw through him
But he didn't care
He loved to watch the ladies
With long or curly hair

He was muscular and strong
I was skinny and weak
Now he can roll the red carpet
At my advocating feet

Past Crimes

"Demjanjuk" killed the Jews
In days of yesteryear
They tried him in these days
Locked him up, do you hear?

Malcolm X's killer
Killed thirty years ago
The law judged him today
No more on the road, you know.

People killed in seventy-nine
In the early eighties, too
So why can't rape crimes
Get justice, and they do?

Rapes of the past are a "crime"
It just happened long ago
The laws were different then
In fact, we did not know.

The man who raped me then
Is still a rapist today
Why pat him on his back
Why give him the praise?

Why let him be free
To mentally rape me now
How can the law be so unfair
How? How? How? How?

"Billy Bailey" killed a man
In nineteen-seventy-nine
The law never forgot him
Today he's paying the time.

Nineteen-eighty-nine
Was John Taylor's year
To commit his murder
Now, people will no more fear.

"Murder" is a crime
And definitely so is "rape"
Let's concentrate on the damage
And not on the "date."

Rape *is* a crime
Traumatic, some can't see
As you read my poems
You'll see what it did to me.

Details (Part I)

Take my hand, I'll give you a hug
I'll comfort you with my scrib
We share the same crime
We share the same pain
We are helping others to live.

We must come together, bond and unite
To show the lawmakers that we are right
Statute of limitations should be permanently removed
So crime victims can finally win the fight.

If your mother was stomped and raped
Would you sit back and take it in stride
Or would you react with questionable concern
To find and punish her attacker, to jail his hide.

Every detail is very important
Every description you must report
Don't hold your tongue, or be afraid to speak
Be frank, be precise, and don't distort.

If your girlfriend was snatched and pushed behind
    subway walls
Or attacked in the public bathroom
Or your fiancée walking home from the mall
Fell prey to a maniac fool.

How would you feel, happy or sad
Would you help her call the police?
Of course you would, you could, and should
So this hood can't escape from the street.

Details (Part II)

Catch every detail you can on his person
His weight, his eyes, any scars
Any disfigurements on his face, the grain of his hair
The color of his skin, the sound of his voice.

Did he have a ring in his ear
Or just an ear that was empty?
Was his hair straight, wavy, nappy
Curly, bald, or scrimpy?

What was the color of his clothes?
Did he have on jeans or a sweatsuit?
Was he dressed in a hooded jacket
Or wearing a heavy plaid sports shirt?

Don't be afraid to talk
Don't be afraid to report
All of this information
Will be very helpful in court.

Your eyes are the camera
Your memory is the brain
The details you give the police
Will place this man in jail.

You can capture the crook
You can pin the creep
You can make sure that
No more he'll walk the street.

Poems

A poem can rhyme
And to rhyme, it doesn't have to
Let's just make beautiful music together
Simply because we need to

A poem can ease
A weary soul at night
Before you fall asleep
Before you rest your sight

A poem can be a doctor
A lawyer, a friend
A poem can be a healer
A therapist to them

A poem can be a teacher
A gift in a note
A poem can be a soother
A cruise on a boat

A poem can be sexy
Degrading or aloof
A poem can be lies
But mostly, they're truths

My poems are meant to educate
So my mistakes are not repeated
An education in rape
A lesson much needed.

Trauma

I've dealt with trauma
My mind shut down for years
Not just one time, but many
Some say I've gone through much
Some say they couldn't take it
Some say they would have broken down a-plenty.

I've dealt with trauma
Not a pleasant trip
But God never promised life to be easy
Some take life for granted
Some take life for a joke
Some take life cheap and sleazy.

Take life for what it is worth
It can be a beautiful thing
You can make life what you want it
Take life for what it's worth
Build a foundation of good deeds
The rewards will be great, you won't regret it.

If you've dealt with trauma
It's not easy to get over it
But life truly must go on
And step by step
It's a mental thing, and you must move on.

The Beast

The smell of his cologne
The slyness of his smile
The cunning of his heart
Led to madness and guile.

The begging of his voice
Asking me to give him some
The demand in his offer
I had no intention of giving him any.

His wood-scented cologne
Of English Leather or Russian
His tie tied so neatly across his chest
He came into bother me
To be a b-e-a-s-t-l-y pest.

His craftiness should have been given a medal
His impeccable smile became a monstrosity
His figure took the form of a v-u-l-t-u-r-e
His two arms became a vice as he gave a bear hug to me.

His lips on my neck
His tongue on my skin
D-i-s-g-u-s-t-e-d me
To the lowest of earthly sins.

I never dreamed the outcome
Of his remarkable goal
Would actually shrink, halt,
And put my life on hold.

I was prey
To a powerful being
Caught like a frightened rabbit
Ready to be skinned.

His arousal was not by my means
He was like a raging dog in heat
The sweat on his forehead, was pouring down
Like a treacherous storm in the street.

Ms. Maya Angelou, and I can relate
No matter how far, or how long was the date

We share something in common, two peas in a pod
The madness, and degrading
A vile act we never forgot.

Solitude

Solitude, solitary confinement
I know very well these three
Being lonely, lonesome, and alone
Being wrapped into myself I'd be,

Stress, headaches, and depression
Weekly visits to therapy
No time for anyone else
I just wanted to take care of me.

I want to be free from this damage
I want to be free from this pain
Must take back control of my life
So I can again start to gainfully gain.

Motivation, dedication, and devotion
Willpower, desire, and goals
Are all the positive things
That will take my life off of "hold."

We will climb the ladder to success
Not necessarilly to riches and fame
I feel we "little people" can conquer
In this life, this treacherous game.

Solitude, solitary confinement
No more locking myself in my room
No more being afraid to go outside
No more living in doom and gloom.

Dark Blue

Does my dark blue leather couch reflect on anything
And the loveseat to match?
My dark blue-striped teacups with the white background

One with a scratch

Do my two dark blue ice chest coolers add some diversity,
Or my dark blue powder compact with a mirror to see?

My dark blue vertical blinds hang so refined in the
Windows, and my dark blue iron kitchen cooking set
By *Le Crueuset*

The dark blue candy dish, which sits on my desk always
Filled with candies, an invitation for my seven grandkids
To indulge goodies into their mouths and tummys.

The dark blue navy childrens' sleeping cots, that have
Soothed a warm child's body many times over and over.

When I go to buy clotheshangers, why are most of them
Dark blue, and if the store has run out of the dark, I'll
Settle for the "other blue"?

Do my dark blue clotheshangers have such an effect on
Me that when my son buys black or another color, I make
Him take them back to the store?

My dark blue baby highchairs look so nice lined together.
But where are the babies, the lovely starry-eyed
Darlings, that sit in them and eat from their dark blue
Three-sectioned plates?

The dark blue laundry detergent is also in this game,
That cleans my whites so bright and with the smell of
Morning dew.

My countless dark blue jars of the only thing I wash my
      face
With, since I was ten years old, Noxzema, "Hello."
Could it be that the navy blue is a reflection of my life?

Truths about Rape

Sixteen percent of rapes are reported
When you tell, don't distort it

Most victims are afraid to report and tell
What they don't understand is he'll go to jail

One out of every seven men are raped
He also is the rapists' bait

Every hour a woman is forced
Beaten, threatened, and coerced

Every single minute, every single day
1,871 women are being sadly raped

Suicide picks a victim's brain
And they play a deadly game

But my friend, it don't have to be
Don't be no fool, 'cause I want you here with me

One out of eight women may kill herself
Because there was no one around to help

Post traumatic stress disorder
You must tell, and you know you ought to

With me, it lasted through many, many years
With me, it lasted through many, many tears
With me, it lasted through many, many fears

Democrat or Republican

An elephant or a donkey
A very diverse pair
A rape or a murder
The crime is still there

Democrat or Republican
A rapist has no respect
It's not a matter of voting
It's not who he'll elect

Catholic, Jewish, or Christian
Muslim or Hindu sect
A rapist is on the prowl
And he cares not whom he'll select

A victim can be male or female
A rapist can be also that
A rapist can be anybody
A rapist can be skinny or fat

Black or white, it doesn't matter
He is not prejudiced
You must be alert and careful
Or he'll have you on his list

A rapist can be a priest
A minister or a bum
He can be a teacher,
A doctor or anyone

Don't ever limit a rapist
To a low life on the street
He can have the best profession
Have you begging at his feet

A rapist is hiding among us
Can you weed him out today?
It is a difficult task
'Cause looks are deceiving, I'll say

It's Christmas, I'm by Myself Again (1995)

If you need a friend
To keep you company
To go to church, lunch, a movie
Please just think of me.

Although I'm earthly lonely
Heavenly love I'll always cling
My Father loves me, this I know
His joy and peace He brings.

I'm not looking to have sex
I'm not looking for a dime
Just to be in "Christian company"
And just to have a nice time.

To come back home elated
From an evening of delight
To ease the pain of loneliness
And to say a clean "Good night."

I'm tired of being lonely
Especially at Christmas Season
Then I think why we celebrate
And I never forget the reason.

We can take time out
To sit at a candle's wick
If you are in doubt
Just call me real quick.

The Stabbing

When they stabbed him in his heart
I couldn't even believe it
He never cursed a word
He never antagonized it.

He was an innocent bystander
He was the only man around
All of my sons were out
In school, or shopping in town.

The blood poured out of his chest
Like nothing I'd seen before
A pillow was placed under his head
The towel was soaked to the core.

The carpet was soaked also
The smell of death in the air
I wished I was having a bad dream
I wish he was not there.

They snatched his life right from under him
A man who worked so hard
To better himself and help others
To help youth with resumes and jobs.

Such a disgrace and waste
Of a life who accomplished so much
He was always a giving person
To everyone he had touched.

Death is always unexpected
So we must always expect it
Never take life for granted
Just because we accept it.

I was traumatized for years
Never wanting to see a kitchen knife
But I had to cut onions and chicken
I needed one in my life.

The ambulance brought a black, zippered bag
As he lay there, eyes toward the ceiling
He never mumbled a word
His life was steadily leaving.

He lay there disbelieving
He saw his life descending
He lay lifeless and motionless
He lay there surely dying.

Every time I hold a knife
I always think of death
I never hold it near me
Lest I fall and hurt myself.

My sister and her new boyfriend
They took my fiancé's life,
So much hate need not be needed
An apology to all, is only right.

I can relate to other mothers
I feel the pain they bore
The grief, the gloom, the madness
The Devil's knife, and life no more.

It was drugs that messed up my sister
Her mind had been warped and changed
She met a guy who did drugs, coke
Now he's doing time behind his name.

My Dad and the Devil

Dad told me boys were devils
To not look at them too long
To not talk to them or be bothered
That to talk to them is wrong.

He threatened me, I couldn't believe it
He told me he'd beat my butt
If he caught me talking to one
If he caught me strutting my stuff.

Dad taught me boys were devils
But he didn't really explain
He thought his teachings were complete
He thought I knew the pain.

Dad told me boys were bad
Said he'd beat me if I talked
To turn my head and ignore them
To just keep walking, walk, and walk.

Later on in life I figured
That Dad only meant good
But educating me on sex
Wasn't as good enough as it should've.

The "birds and bees," he said
Don't do what they do in the trees
But Dad should've been more frank
And Mom should've taught poor me

I learned from the girls in the cafeteria
I learned from the girls in the bathroom
I saw writings on the walls and the tables
The education was in the washrooms.

I saw drawings of a penis and vagina
I saw words of how good "it" felt
I saw the reality of what Dad meant
But he taught it by the fear of his belt.

Thank goodness we lived to the nineties
Where education is on the front burner
We've come a long way, Daddy
And we are better learners.

I'm Glad You're Going to Heaven

I looked long and hard for an answer
Dark, deep, dank days I loved
I sought counseling, medication
Hospitals were not my dig

The only thing that could help me
Was over my head above
It came to me by spirit
The salvation of God's love

Oh, sweet reward, sweet joy
Sweet Jesus, and sweet gladness
In Him you find only happiness
No doom or gloom or sadness

It's hard to change some people
To try and turn them around
Until they're on their deathbed
And then they'll say, they want to be Heaven-bound

Better late than never, my friend
'Cause "the Lord" will hear your plea
I'm glad you're going to Heaven
'Cause then you'll see jolly old me

My Smokey Joe's Cafe

At this point and time
I have a son of mine
Who smokes, and smokes, and smokes

No New Year's resolution
He fills himself with pollution
Can you help me to save his life?

My mother died of cancer
Smoked three packs a day
I couldn't convince her to quit

She was loving and sweet
I loved her to death
And now "Joe" is going the same way

I hear the warnings
In papers and T.V.
In journals and medical reports

I feel he will blame me
One day for his illness
How stubborn can a person be?

To walk in the house
And smell his smoke
I have much care and concern

His opened window
Won't save his life
And I feel it's not a joke

Cancer Society
Is there a picture you can send me
To show and prove it to my Joe

To convince him to quit
To help save his life
Please help us, I beg you, my friend.

With a bottle of beer
He feels no fear
I can assure him he will
When his lungs get sick
And his kidneys fail
Then he will learn to adhere

I knew it would happen
My Smokey Joe's Cafe
In his room, this son of mine

At this juncture and time
This son "Joe," I call mine
I love him, that I cry

If he loves his mother
He'll care enough
To at least, slow down a little bit at a time

It's like a slow time bomb
This cancer so deadly
Toxins eating away his insides

He says he has to die from something
Please, there are no excuses
To play Russian Roulette like a medley

The Cracks of the City

The cracks of the city
Oh, what a pity
I am under one now

The cracks of the city
Are not very pretty
I'm stuck and I know why

And I'll find my way
Some upcoming day
And it won't be too long

I'll dust myself off
And again I will walk
And I will sing my song

The cracks of the city
Where it's very gritty
Is not for me to stay

The cracks of the city
I cannot breathe
I will find some fresh air one day

The cracks of the city
My time has come
To get me back up there
A spiritual awakening
God has planted in my weary soul

He keeps me strong
He gives me strength
To climb out of this hole

The cracks of domestic abuse and rape
The cracks of lies, conceit, and hate

The cracks of loneliness, solitude, and moods
Depression and pain, all kinds of abuse

The cracks of the city

Bullets Passing by My Window

Bullets passing by my window
When will it ever cease
When can I stop ducking and dodging
To begin to seek some peace?

Is this the way I'll die
Or even be permanently maimed?
Bullets passing by my window
If I'm hit, who'll be to blame?

I stand in front of my dresser
Two twin mirrors stand upright
Gold trimmed brass so pretty
But I fear the bullet's bite.

Will it hit me in my head
As I roll up my hair at night
Or will it hit me in the heart
A terribly gruesome sight.

Will it travel and hit my doorknob
Ricochet and hit the brass
Make a U-turn in the wink of an eye
And make a hit so fast?

I always fear the bullet's lead
The thought ripping open my skin
The blood pours out like a fountain
As the warm air slowly sets in.

I lie in my bed and curl right up
With my arms protecting my head
I curl right up into a fetal position
Hoping the bullet won't make me dead.

I shrink and I squirm
I cannot sleep a wink
It takes me some hours to get calm
And to finally fall asleep.

I listen for fireworks and horns
On a lively New Year's Day
Instead, I get the sound
Of bullets passing my way.

In the middle of the year
They come and they go
They are a menace and disgrace
To everyday people who know.

They are so small and deadly
But have no mind of their own
They are swift and sleek, and shiny
Another demise from the Devil, when it hits home.

Being on Welfare

Being on welfare is no joke,
You're always scrambling, you're always broke.
Your kids need sneakers, and you need shoes,
You're always crying the "I'm broke blues."

Life in the ghetto, life in the streets,
Life that no mother should have to meet.
Always hungry, hand forever out,
If your check don't come, you've reason to pout.

Caught up in the system, can't get away,
You try to find a job, but it's itsy-bitsy pay.
Rent time is due, and you're $50.00 short,
No one to borrow, so you're taken to court.

Can't see Broadway plays, so you watch T.V.,
Living in fantasy world, is all it's gonna be.
Can't get respect, from "those other folk,"
Having to wear hand-me-downs, is no joke.

Don't ever let no man, tell you he got good stuff,
You must be a fighter, stand tall and tough.
Times are a-changing, and you must too,
Let no man stop you, else you'll be blue.

Got no insurance, no money to build,
Even dying is a shame, if you go to Potter's Field.
Welfare is a way of life, chronic it may come,
I myself don't ever wish this life on no one.

Being on welfare is like having the plague,
Begging for an S.O.S., waving a white flag.
Searching for an answer, looking for a goal,
Hoping one day, they'll help a weary soul.

Always full of anger, always full of stress,
No matter what you do, it's not your total best.
They tease you in the morning, they tease you in the dawn,
They mock your insecurity, when you die, they don't even
    mourn.

Don't let temptation bring you, to its lowest degree,
To drugs, and sex, and lust, to total dependency.
You can't shop at A&S, your money is too low,
Credit cards you have none, basement bargains aglow.

Buying the cheapest clothes, wearing plastic shoes,
When leather and snakeskin are things you'll never use.
You can fight the system, you can alter change,
You can be a winner, you can change your name.

Take time to wonder, take time to think,
Educate yourself my friend, advancement on the brink.
Life must go on, as I search for better ways
And hope God will let me see, and have better days.

My First Racial Encounter

When my father drove down south
To visit Grandma and Pa
The scenery was green and beautiful
We stayed inside our car.

My father at times was tired
But he had to sweat it out
Alone he drove all the way
Did not complain a lot.

His family was his priority
Our lives were in his hands
I became nervous and bothered
The mountain's height I could not stand.

My dad at times stopped the car
Because he had to p——
We drove up to a gas station
They told him to find a tree.

That's the first time I experienced
The power of a racist heart
I felt sad for my daddy
Saw him disappear behind a piece of bark.

A car hit us from the side
But we was in the deep South
The white man said it was our fault
The white cop told Dad to shut his mouth.

It was raining cats and dogs
They told Dad to follow them
The rain was heavy and blinding
Dad made a U-turn, disappeared down a bend.

We were afraid, but laughed
Dad was not ready to go to jail
We prayed the rain would not stop
We escaped from the Devil's fate.

Stuck-Up People

You walk with your head stuck up to the sky
Your nose has stretched there also
You turn your head when I try to speak
You act like I'm a person you don't know.

You pass by in your car, never wave a hand
Never nod your head "good day"
When you see me coming, you play dumbfounded
Hate to see me approaching your way.

Why do you hate me, I never did you any harm
I have tried to be your friend
You try your best to turn against me
You've tried until the end.

Why do you work so hard to be unfriendly?
Was it taught to you as a child?
Why don't you try to have a heart
So one day we can chat a while?

Can saying hello be so difficult
When you see me in the street
What makes you think I'm not your worth
We came from the same beat.

If you prefer to be cold, that's fine
If you prefer not to speak, that's OK
But remember my friend of tight-lip syndrome
You may need me to help you one day.

Do you think you are so fine, so bad
Too pretty, too clean, or what?
You look no better than anyone else
You're just dirt, from the earth, all dressed up.

Earth has given us many things
Almost everything we own
At the end of your life, you'll know it better
When you return to the dust, no more to roam.

Determination

Why must I grow old
And read my poems to myself?
Why can't they be placed
Upon many a different shelf?

Why must poverty
Claim my place in lights?
Why can't they agree
Raise me to higher heights?

"Poor" does not mean stupid
"Less" does not mean dumb
Talents and gifts from God
Are scattered through everyone

Survival of the fittest
Is what they do say
If you can't survive the poverty
We must stay down in disgrace

But I refuse to stay
In an atmosphere of decay
The cracks of the city
Is not my plan this day

I am full of words
I am brimming over the top
God has blessed me with these poems
I must say, I cannot stop

So why treat me like a dumbbell
I know well I can do better
I have tried to reach the readers
With many a pen and letter

I do not write about politics
On history or math
I speak on a rape
That's torn my life in half

I also mean to teach
To show and educate
I write these poems of "healing"
To which my life I dedicate.

Fellow in My Dreams

From 1985 to the present time, you see
There's a person in my life, but he's only in my dreams.

I don't understand the message it implies
But I hope I find out, before I up and die.

At first I didn't feel anything
I chalked it up as just a dream
But the fellow kept popping up
Do you know what I mean?

After two dreams or three
It didn't really bother me
But after ten, fifteen and twenty
It bothered me plenty.

I said, "God" must be behind it
I cannot question "God's" ways
This fellow was always distant
In real life, until recent days.

Last night, I dreamed again
And he was surely there
March 16, 1996
These dreams cause concerns and care.

This guy is five years younger
A devout Christian church-goer
He pays his tithes on time
He's a Devil whistle-blower.

I say to myself in awe
This ceases to amaze me
The dreams of him keep coming
So many, it nearly dazes me.

Such a phenomenal occurrence
Only I can ponder on
The mystery of his presence
Is always there, never gone.

Will he ever go away?
Always invading me
A mystery in disguise
This fellow in my dreams.